MW00876512

How to F
SUCCESSFULLY
Groom Your Doodle At Home

(For the Cheapskate Doodle Owner)

By Professional Pet Groomer
Desiree Bee Plant
over 77 five star Yelp Reviews

Includes secrets of the grooming trade without having to attend a grooming school

Table of Contents

The Tools You Need to Groom Your Doodle

Hello Fellow Cheapskate Doodle Dog Owner!

I have created this book just for you and your beloved pet. Maybe you don't trust any groomer with your doodle, maybe you have had some bad haircuts and are sick of overpaying for them, whatever the reason, I have the solution for you within this book.

In order to be successful at home grooming your doodle, and doing a good job, you must listen to me when I tell you, "Good Grooming Tools" are first and foremost important.

If you purchased a easy do-it-yourself pet grooming kit, and it has one screwed on blade and a bunch of combs, I am sorry to tell you, that will not do. Those are not designed to cut through your doodle's massive coat and even if it does and your convinced that it's the tool, I am telling you-you must invest in good tools if you want to do a good job on your doodle.

First thing you need is a metal "greyhound" comb. I recommend getting the one with very small teeth that goes to the larger teeth. The very first step to grooming your doodle at home is the preparation work, and this comb is your guide to finding the knots and tangles so you can eventually clip through the hair with ease.

Once you have your comb, you will need an A-5 clipper. I use Andis Two Speed personally because they are lightweight and run for a long time. These clippers will run you about $150 and usually always include a number 10 blade with the packaging. If you do not purchase this type of clipper, you will not be successful in your home grooming.

The Grooming Blades I have suggested in this chapter are for the most traditional Doodle looks. For a majority of Doodle owners, they do no want their dogs to look like a "poodle", instead they prefer a shaggier dog.

Because of this, I am recommending a number 30 blade and a set of snap on metal grooming combs. If for whatever reason your A-5 clipper did not come with a 10 blade, please purchase it.

In addition to the previous tools listed, you will need a slicker brush, and a pair of thinning shears. Since you pay for what you get, I highly recommend paying upwards of over $60 for a good pair of sharp double teeth thinning shears.

When shaving the underneath of the pads, most groomers can use a 10 blade, in my experience the dogs usually don't like how large the blade is in between their feet. I recommend for this job a small "peanut" hair trimmer, which can be found at any grooming supply outlet.

Overview of tools needed

1. Greyhound Comb
2. A-5 Clipper
3. 10 blade and 30 blade
4. Set of metal snap on combs
5. Slicker Brush
6. Double Teeth Thinning Shears
7. Peanut Hair Trimmer
8. Grooming Noose

It is recommended to keep the tools in a safe water proof container or toolbox. If your tools are kept in good condition they could last a couple years easily.

Try not to drop the scissors or clippers on the ground while grooming as you could easily break them.

Creating a Safe Place to Successfully Groom Your Doodle

Investing in a grooming table is your best bet for a quality job. Being bent over on the ground while grooming your doodle can easily cause injury to your back. A standard grooming table goes for about $100 and can be found online.

If your Doodle happens to be under 20 pounds you may want a table that goes to your belly button. Most standard, cheap grooming tables work fine for Doodles. Just make sure it comes with a grooming arm and a grooming noose.

Don't ever leave your dog on your grooming table, they could hang themselves in seconds, leaving you with a horrible tragedy. I recommended for hyper dogs to take them for a long walk before grooming them, so they can be more still.

Using a quiet room with no distractions is the best way to groom your pet. If you have a table you want to use to groom your dog, you can insert an eye hook into a stud in the wall and have your dog tethered to that while you groom. I do recommend using an actual grooming table, but if your looking to cut corners you can use this method as well.

A showerhead is recommended while prepping the dog in the bathtub. You want to make sure the dog can be properly rinsed off and not retain any shampoo.

Preparation of Dog's Coat

So this maybe the most "important" part of this book. If you cannot completely comb your Doodle out with your greyhound metal comb, then you may have to take your pet to the professional groomers for a shave down and start fresh.

In order to successfully groom your Doodle you must be a superhero when it comes to maintaining your Doodle's coat. It does not have to be brushed everyday, but you do have to be responsible and diligently comb your dog from the tip of his mustache, behind each ear, underneath his chest, to the very end of his tail. The reason being, you can't have a patchy looking pup, shaving out matts can be unslightly so I recommended starting fresh. If you are reading this book and cannot get the tangles out of your Doodle-go to a groomer and have the coat sheared and revisit this book when your pups hair is long enough.

Once you get your Doodle completely combed out you are ready for the serious prep work!

Having a quality brand of shampoo that gentle suds away all the dirt is key to a beautiful coat. I always let the dog sit in the shampoo for about 5 minutes and work a later into their fur. On their faces I use a "tearless" shampoo that I can scrub all their crusties with.

After a good shampoo, I like to use a thick dog conditioner. The only problem that can arise is if you do not wash the conditioner out. Hair that still has conditioner on it will take FOREVER to dry. To be safe always double rinse your Doodle and make sure you don't miss any spots.

To save time on drying your Doodle, use several towels to dry your pet. The more water you can squeeze off your pet, the better. You do not want any soaking wet parts. For example a properly towel dried Doodle should take 10 minutes to squeeze out and probably two big bath sized towels.

Once your Doodle is towel dried to satisfaction, place the damp towels on the grooming table and put your pup onto and secure them with the grooming noose.

Take your hair dryer on a warm/cool setting and keep it 5 inches from the skin-be mindful not to burn your pet. With your slicker brush, gently brush the hair as the air hits it, drying it straight.

Drying your Doodle will take up to an hour or more depending on the length of the hair and size of your dog. If you feel you need a faster blow dry method, they make "force" dryers, but I am not recommending it for the faint of heart. Your Doodle may try to fly off the grooming table because of the loudness of the force dryer. If you feel that you want to work with your pet on the ground first and train them to deal with the loudness of the force dryer, it can easily cut drying time in half.

Once your beloved Doodle is dried, you must take out your greyhound comb and comb every single inch of your pet, I mean it, every single inch of your Doodle! If you find a few matts you can try to take the slicker brush to them and then slowly pick through them with the greyhound comb. The reason being is because the snap on clipper combs will sharply come off if they encounter a matt, and it could scare your dog into -yes you guessed it-flying off the grooming   table!!

Different Styles of Doodle Cuts

The long shaggy Teddy Bear Look

This seems to be everyone's favorite of all the Doodle owners. This pup definitely doesn't look like a poodle, at all.

So to be honest, this is a hard look to maintain. If your Doodle gets wet and doesn't get completely combed out, the tangles are almost immediate and they are seemingly invisible if you don't use your greyhound comb to find them.

To achieve this look you use your largest snap on attachment. First attach the 30 blade to your clippers and then the largest comb attachment. You are going to hold the clippers like a pencil and move downwards with the hair, not upwards.

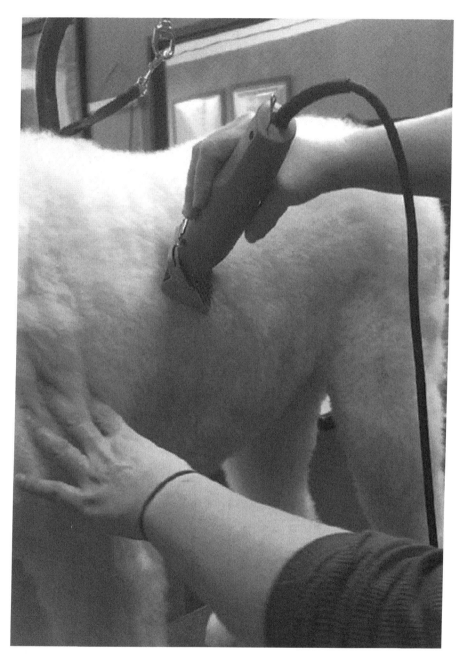

There are two ways to taper this look more, you can be creative and leave the legs longer than the body or you can do the body all the same length. To leave the legs longer, simply use a larger comb, either one or two sizes smaller on the body.

Do not use the smaller combs on the legs and longer on the body, it would make your dog look silly and uneven.

Once you have used the clippers, go over your pet with the slicker brush and comb the hair backwards so it sticks up. This is called " Back brushing".

Repeat the clip with the clippers. This helps to get a more even cut. If you can still see uneven hairs, repeat steps as much as possible.

When doing the face, you can either use a comb on the entire dog, or use your thinning shears to "shape the face".

Using the largest comb on the face creates a cute face

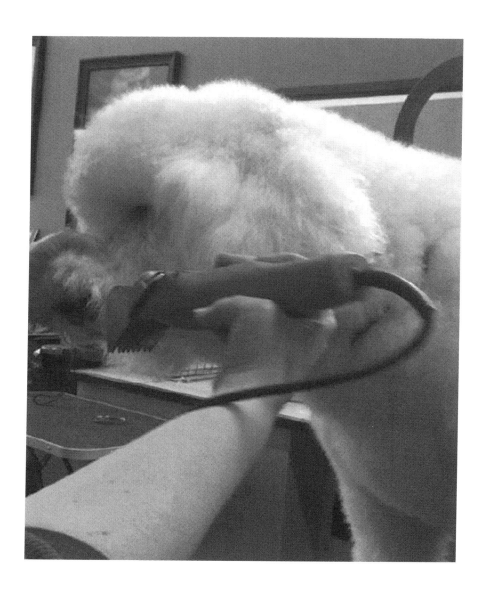

Always go "downwards" with the clippers, be careful of the eyes!

The "Still Fluffy But Shorter" Doodle Cut

For those of you who don't want to obsessively comb your doodle every week, this haircut is for you!

This is 5/8 comb attachment on the body with a ¾ on the face. The ears can be done as short as ½ comb or longer depending on how long you want the pups ears to look.

The Short Doodle Cut

Okay cheapskates, this cut is for you! You love your Doodle, but you don't love grooming it all the time, and you don't care for all the soggy wet hair either.

Snap on your ¼ comb shave away. Remember to always go downward on your dog's hair and not upward. (refer to picture on how to hold clippers)

If you would like the face to be longer, feel free to use up to a ½ comb, be wary not to poke your dog in the eyes! Ears can be done with the ¼ attachment comb for super short look.

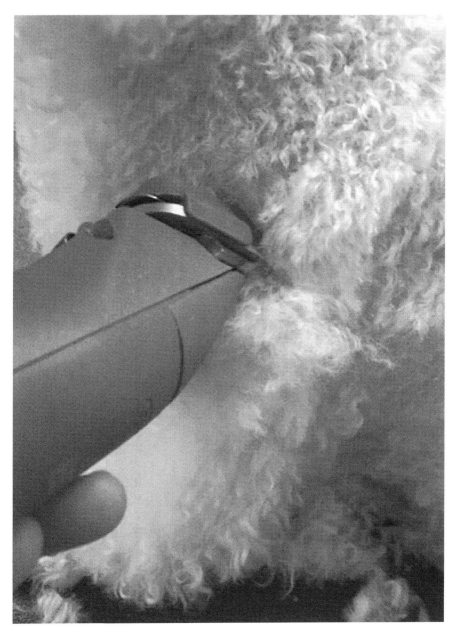

How to Shave out the underneath of the Paws

With your peanut trimmer, gently hold your dog's paw and simply shave out all the hair between the toes.

This is a very sensitive area, so go really slow and use the clippers to dig out the hair in the V of the foot.

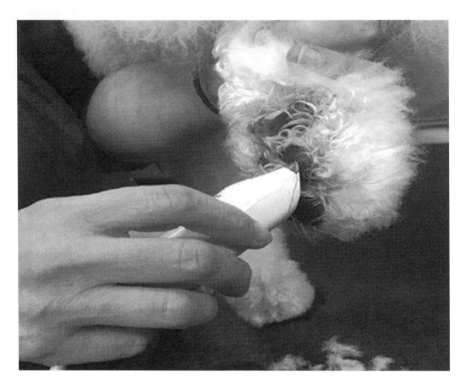

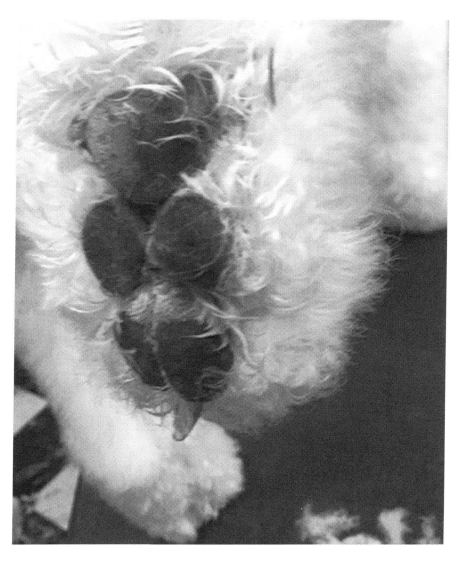

How to do your Doodle's Sanitary trim

Snap on your 10 blade. First rule of thumb-do not let this blade get HOT. It will burn your pet's privates and that would not be cool.

Do not shave OVER the ANUS. You may shave around it, but do not shave OVER it. Ideally the sanitary is shaving around the anus and around the vulva, and penis.

You want to be really gentle and patient when shaving these areas. Depending on what you prefer you may want to do a little trimming, or a lot. Make sure your dog's penis is retracted safely into it's sheath before shaving around his penis.

The 10 blade is a safe blade, however you want to always check to see if it is warm or hot and you want to hold your clippers gently and let the clippers "eat" the hair around the privates, not forcefully press the clippers into the skin.

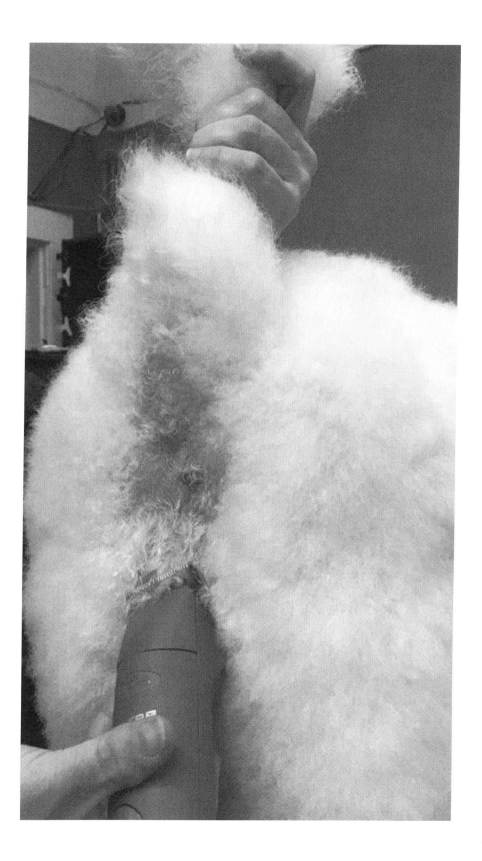

Scissor Handling and Angles

It is important to hold your thinning shears with your ring finger and your thumb. Doing this provides a wider range of cut.

When using the thinning shears, I always recommended a correctly washed and blow dried coat. Using the greyhound comb, simply comb the hair outward and use the shears to even out any spots the clipper may have left.

The thinning shears are relatively safe shears, however you can cut a dog's skin if you are not careful. When trimming out tangles in a dog's coat, thinning shears can help lessen the hairloss, just don't pull the matt, as it will pull the skin. If the skin is pulled, it can easily be cut by the thinning shears. It is always a better idea to try to use a slicker brush first, then a greyhound comb to pick through the knot.

When handling the scissors, it is a good idea to hold them at the angle best suited for the trim. See the following pictures.

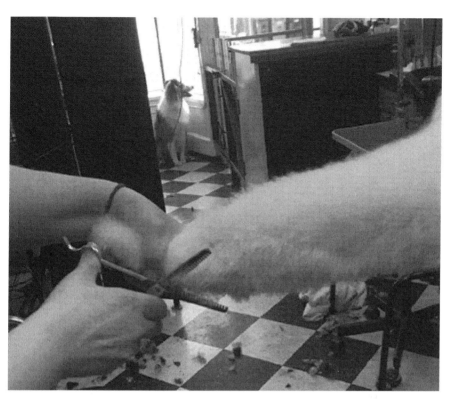

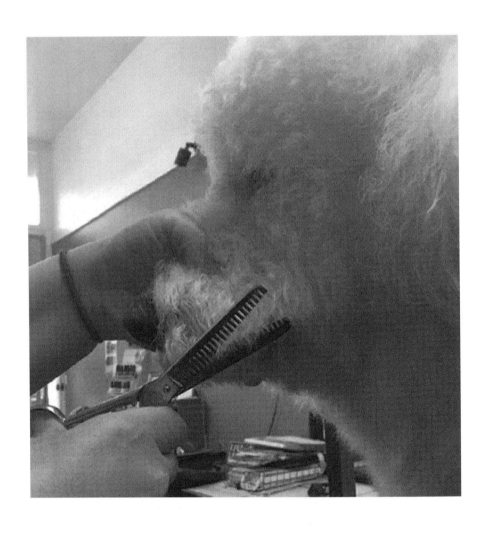

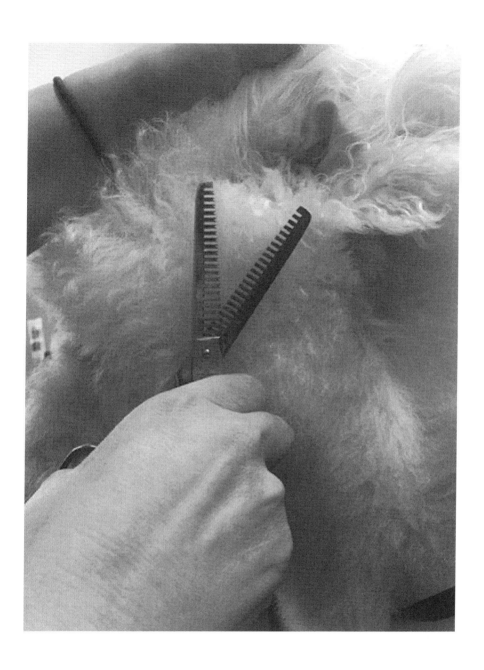

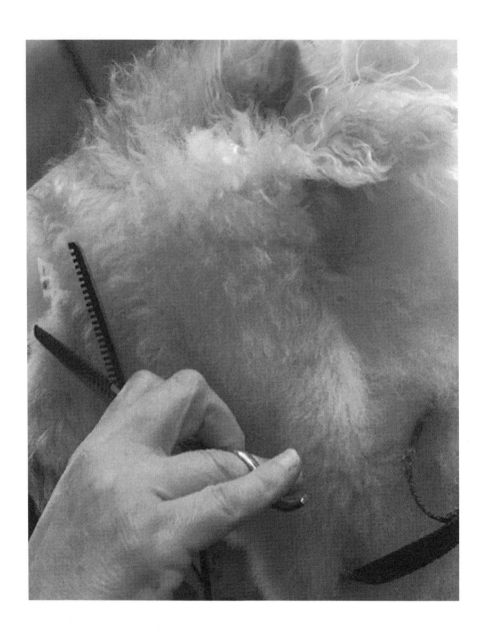

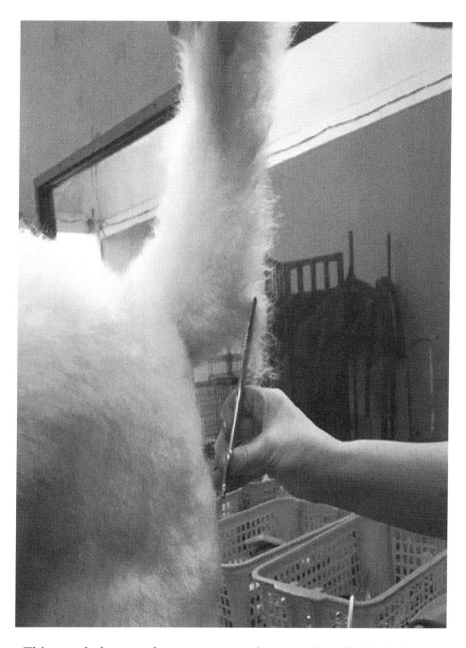

This concludes your lesson on grooming your Doodle! Enjoy!

Made in the USA
Middletown, DE
03 February 2022

60354219R00019